Table of Contents

Chapter 1: Introduction

Welcome

You are invited to "The Procrastination Trap: Why We Delay and How to Take Control." If you've picked up this book, you've probably experienced the irritating cycle of procrastination. You are not alone, and there is potential for a more productive future.

The Scope of Procrastination

Procrastination affects everyone at some time, but understanding why it occurs and how to overcome it is critical to gaining control of your life and reaching your objectives. This book will walk you through the process of determining the fundamental causes of your procrastination and present practical suggestions for taking action.

Chapter 2:
Understanding Procrastination

The Definition of Procrastination

Procrastination is the act of delaying or postponing tasks while knowing the negative repercussions. It is a typical behavior that can cause stress, anxiety, and feelings of unfulfillment.

Common Myths and Misconceptions

There are numerous myths regarding procrastinating. Some blame sloth or bad time management, but the truth is typically more complicated. Understanding the underlying nature of procrastination is the first step towards overcoming it.

The Science Behind Procrastination

Recent research in psychology and neuroscience has offered insight on why people procrastinate. Understanding the science, from brain chemistry to behavioral patterns, can aid in the development of successful procrastination strategies.

Chapter 3:
The Psychological Roots of Procrastination

Fear of Failure

Fear of failure can be paralyzing, causing us to put off tasks to avoid potential negative outcomes. Learning to reframe failure as a learning opportunity is crucial for overcoming this barrier.

Perfectionism

Perfectionism can lead to procrastination because the fear of not doing something perfectly can prevent us from starting at all. Embracing a mindset of progress over perfection can help.

Decision Fatigue

Making decisions can be mentally exhausting, leading to procrastination. Simplifying choices and developing routines can reduce decision fatigue and increase productivity.

Lack of Motivation

Motivation fluctuates, and waiting for it to strike can lead to endless delays. Understanding how to cultivate and maintain motivation is key to taking consistent action.

Chapter 4:
The Impact of Procrastination

On Mental Health

Procrastination can cause increased tension, anxiety, and feelings of guilt. Recognizing the influence on mental health can be a powerful incentive for action.

On Relationships

Procrastination can cause problems in relationships with friends, family, and colleagues. Learning to manage your time more effectively can enhance your interactions and build your relationships.

On Career and Personal Goals

Procrastination can stymie career growth and impede you from meeting personal objectives. Developing proactive behaviors can help you maximize your potential.

Chapter 5: Identifying Your Procrastination Triggers

Self-Assessment Quiz

Helps readers identify their procrastination triggers. Examples of inquiries are, "Do you frequently put off starting tasks because they appear overwhelming?" Alternatively, "Do you frequently miss deadlines?"

Common Triggers and Patterns

Common triggers include task aversion, lack of clarity, and contextual influences. For example, a crowded desk may encourage procrastination.

Personal Reflection Exercises

Readers are guided through exercises designed to help them reflect on their procrastinating behaviors. Journaling about recent experiences of procrastination can help identify underlying issues.

Self-Assessment Quiz: Identify Your Procrastination Triggers

Instructions:
Answer each question honestly. Use the scale below to rate how frequently each statement applies to you:

- 1 = Never
- 2 = Rarely
- 3 = Sometimes
- 4 = Often
- 5 = Always

1. Task Aversion

- I postpone starting things that I find uninteresting or unpleasant.
- I avoid tasks that are difficult or intricate.
- I put off jobs that do not interest me, even if they are important.

2. Fear of Failure

- I put off starting tasks because I am afraid I won't complete them well.
- I avoid tasks because I am frightened to make blunders.
- I postpone because I am concerned about being judged by others.

3. Perfectionism

- I procrastinate because I want to complete tasks precisely.
- I spend a long time perfecting details before moving on.
- I put off finishing chores because they are not "good enough" yet.

4. Decision Fatigue

- I'm overwhelmed by the number of decisions I need to make.
- I postponed making judgments until the last minute.
- I avoid projects requiring a lot of decision-making.

5. Lack of Motivation

- I struggle to find inspiration to begin tasks, even if they are vital.
- I wait for inspiration or motivation to strike before I begin working.
- I find it difficult to stay motivated during a task.

6. Distractions

- I'm easily sidetracked by my phone, social media, and other things.
- I procrastinate by completing less important chores instead.
- I have trouble focusing on projects without getting diverted.

7. Time Management

- I frequently underestimate how long projects will take.
- I often run out of time to complete assignments.
- I postpone chores until the deadline is really close.

8. Procrastination Habits

- I often check my email or social media instead of working.
- I tell myself "I'll do it later" and then don't.
- I frequently feel guilty or stressed for not starting activities sooner.

Scoring:
Add up your scores for each section

- **Task Aversion:**
  __ / 15
- **Fear of Failure:**
  __ / 15
- **Perfectionism:**
  __ / 15
- **Decision Fatigue:**
  __ / 15
- **Lack of Motivation:**
  __ / 15
- **Distractions:**
  __ / 15
- **Time Management:**
  __ / 15
- **Procrastination Habits:**
  __ / 15

Interpreting Your Scores:

10-15:

- This area is a significant trigger for your procrastination. Focus on strategies to address these issues.

6-9:

- This area occasionally contributes to your procrastination. Be mindful of these triggers and work on mitigating them.

1-5:

- This area is less of a trigger for your procrastination. Maintain your current habits but be aware of potential issues.

Chapter 6: Strategies to Overcome Procrastination

Goal-Setting and Planning

Teaches effective goal-setting approaches, such as SMART goals (Specific, Measurable, Achievable, Relevant, and Time-bound). One example would be to divide a major project into smaller, more manageable jobs with set deadlines.

Time Management Techniques

Investigates approaches such as the Eisenhower Matrix to prioritize jobs and time blocking to set out particular times for focused work. One example is setting apart designated hours for intensive work and breaks.

Developing a Proactive Mindset

Discusses how to cultivate a proactive mindset by prioritizing long-term goals and breaking down activities into actionable actions. For example, imagining the successful completion of a project might help inspire daily development.

Using Technology for Your Advantage

Recommended productivity tools and apps, such as Trello for task management and Focus@Will for concentration. Examples include using Trello boards to track progress and utilizing Pomodoro timer applications.

Chapter 7:
Behavioral Techniques

Breaking Down Tasks into Smaller Steps

Explains how breaking down activities into smaller, more achievable steps can lessen overwhelm and enhance the likelihood of getting started. For example, instead of writing the complete report, concentrate on drafting the introduction.

The Pomodoro Technique

Introduces the Pomodoro Technique, which consists of working in focused intervals (often 25 minutes) followed by brief pauses. One example is using a timer to complete a task in 25 minutes and then taking a 5-minute break.

Reward Systems
Setting up incentive systems can motivate work completion. For example, give yourself a treat after completing a difficult work.

Accountability Partners
Explains the advantages of using an accountability buddy to keep on track. One example is to check in with a friend or coworker on a regular basis to see how things are doing with joint goals.

Chapter 8:
Cognitive Approaches

Cognitive Behavioral Therapy (CBT)

Aims to identify and change problematic thought habits. For example, presenting evidence of previous triumphs to challenge the belief "I'll never finish this".

Mindfulness & Meditation

Explores how mindfulness and meditation can aid in being present and focused. Guided meditation activities can help reduce anxiety and enhance concentration.

Reframe Negative Thoughts

Teaches how to recast negative beliefs into good ones. For example, "This task is too hard" could be replaced by "This task is challenging but manageable."

Developing Self-Compassion

Investigates how self-compassion can decrease self-criticism and boost resilience. Examples include practicing self-kindness and acknowledging that everyone struggles with procrastination on occasion.

Chapter 9:
Creating a Productive Environment

Decluttering Your Space

Explains how a clutter-free workplace can improve productivity. For example, organize your desk and remove any superfluous stuff to create a clean workstation.

Minimizing Distractions

Discusses ways for reducing distractions, such as turning off notifications and creating boundaries. One example is the use of website blockers to prevent access to distracting websites during work hours.

Designing an Inspirational Workspace

Provides advice on how to create an inspirational and motivating workplace. Plants, artwork, and a vision board are some examples of things you can add to your workstation.

Chapter 10: Maintaining Momentum

Celebrating Small Wins
Encourages recognizing little accomplishments to keep motivated. For example, recognize and celebrate the completion of each chapter of a writing project.

Dealing with Setbacks
Provides ideas for overcoming setbacks and remaining resilient. Examples include viewing setbacks as learning opportunities and devising a strategy for getting back on track.

Long-Term Strategies for Sustainable Action
discusses long-term productivity strategies. For example, schedule regular review sessions to analyze progress and change goals.

Chapter 11:
Real-Life Success Stories

Case Studies for Overcoming Procrastination

Provides case studies of people who have effectively overcome procrastination. Examples include a student who improved their grades by developing new study habits or an entrepreneur who expanded their firm by employing time management tactics.

Interviews with Productivity Experts

Includes conversations with productivity specialists who share their thoughts and approaches. Authors, psychologists, and business executives have all provided suggestions into overcoming procrastination.

Inspirational Quotes and Insights

Offers motivating quotations and insights from successful people. Famous authors, athletes, and entrepreneurs have all expressed the significance of taking action.